Teaching Little Fingers to Play

Jazz and Rock
Piano Solos With Optional Teacher Accompaniments

by
Eric Baumgartner

CONTENTS

Cover Design by Nick Gressle

12418

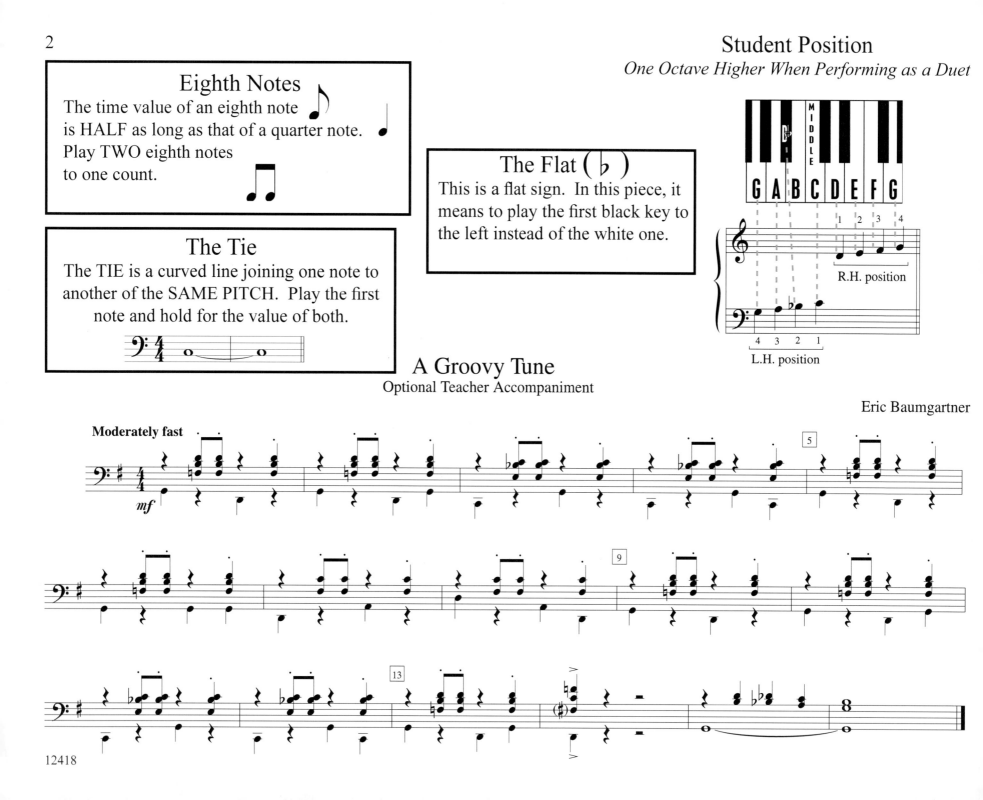

Eighth Notes

The time value of an eighth note is HALF as long as that of a quarter note. Play TWO eighth notes to one count.

The Tie

The TIE is a curved line joining one note to another of the SAME PITCH. Play the first note and hold for the value of both.

The Flat (♭)

This is a flat sign. In this piece, it means to play the first black key to the left instead of the white one.

Student Position
One Octave Higher When Performing as a Duet

R.H. position

L.H. position

A Groovy Tune
Optional Teacher Accompaniment

Eric Baumgartner

Moderately fast

mf

A Groovy Tune

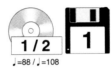

Play both hands one octave higher when performing as a duet.

Eric Baumgartner

12418

Doo Wop at the Sock Hop

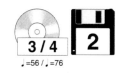

Play as written when performing as a duet.

Eric Baumgartner

50's style rock

snap fingers or slap thigh

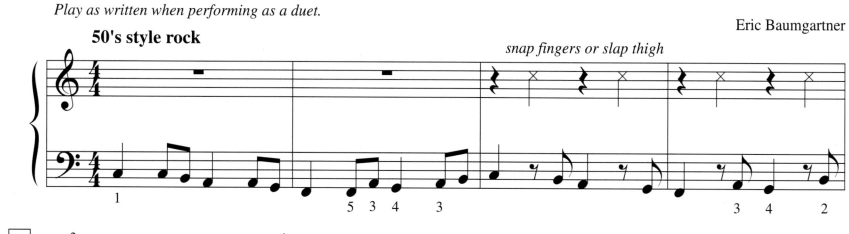

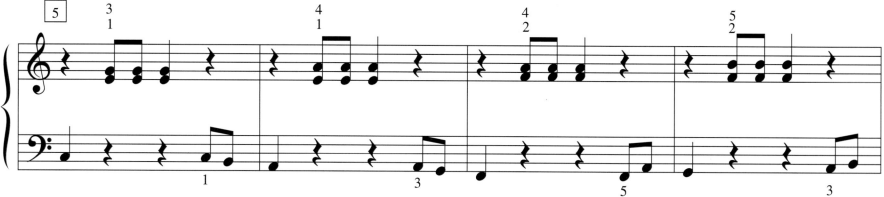

12418

Rests

In music notation there are SIGNS of SILENCE, called RESTS, which tell us when and for how long our fingers should be silent.

Quarter Rest 𝄽 = 1 count

Whole Rest* ▬ = 4 counts

Eighth Rest 𝄾 = 1/2 count

*The WHOLE REST receives the counts for the whole measure indicated by the top number of the time signature.

Student Position
Play As Written When Performing as a Duet

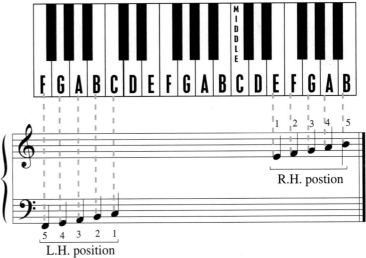

Doo Wop at the Sock Hop
Optional Teacher Accompaniment

Eric Baumgartner

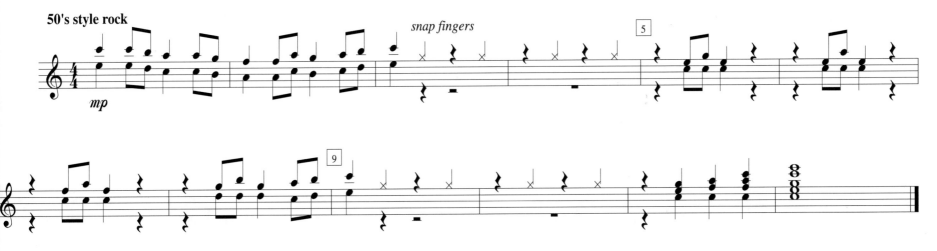

6

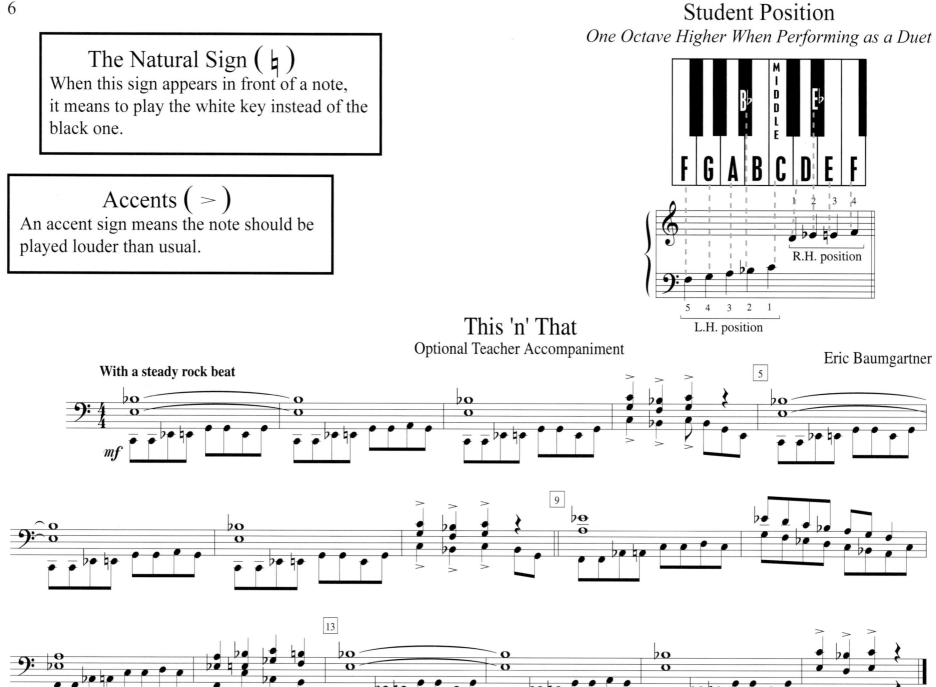

The Natural Sign (♮)
When this sign appears in front of a note, it means to play the white key instead of the black one.

Accents (>)
An accent sign means the note should be played louder than usual.

Student Position
One Octave Higher When Performing as a Duet

This 'n' That
Optional Teacher Accompaniment

Eric Baumgartner

With a steady rock beat

This 'n' That

Play both hands one octave higher when performing as a duet.

Eric Baumgartner

With a steady rock beat

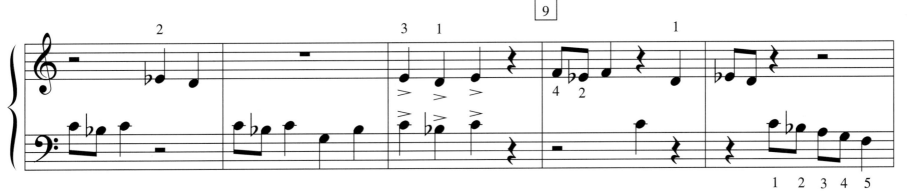

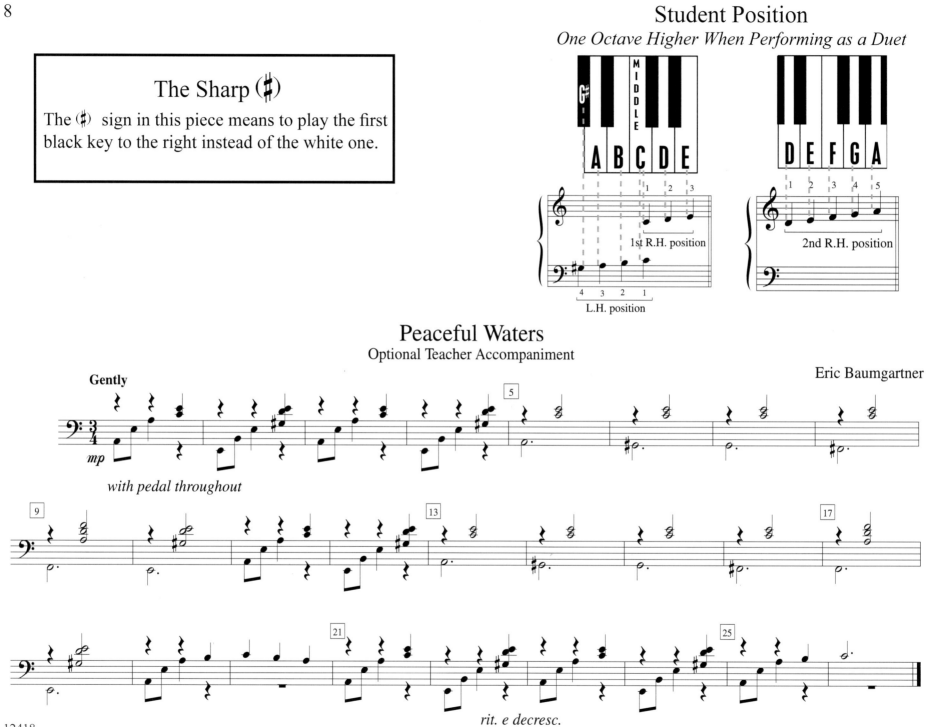

8

The Sharp (♯)

The (♯) sign in this piece means to play the first black key to the right instead of the white one.

Student Position
One Octave Higher When Performing as a Duet

1st R.H. position

L.H. position

2nd R.H. position

Peaceful Waters
Optional Teacher Accompaniment

Eric Baumgartner

Gently

mp

with pedal throughout

rit. e decresc.

12418

Peaceful Waters

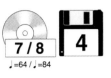

Play both hands one octave higher when performing as a duet.

Eric Baumgartner

Gently

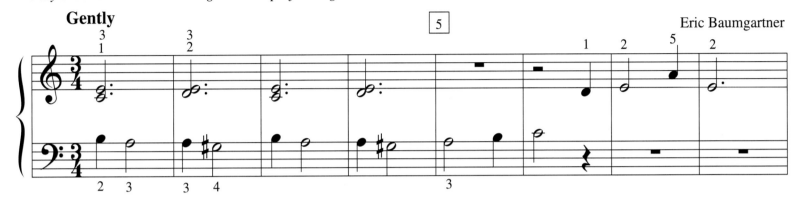

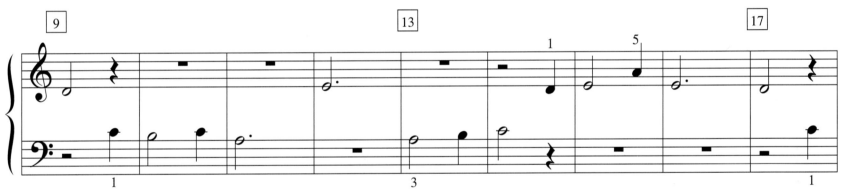

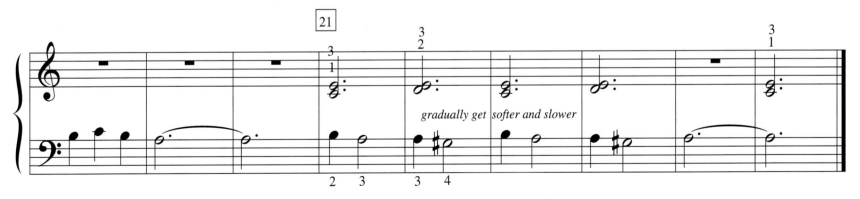

gradually get softer and slower

Student Position
One Octave Higher When Performing as a Duet

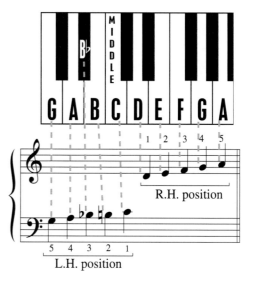

12 Bar Blues
Notice that this song has 12 measures. Many Rock, Jazz and Blues pieces are written this way. Can you find other pieces in this collection with 12 measures?

Camel Caravan
Optional Teacher Accompaniment

Eric Baumgartner

Not too fast

Camel Caravan

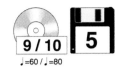

Eric Baumgartner

Play both hands one octave higher when performing as a duet.

Not too fast

Two Names For The Same Black Key

D♯ and E♭ are the same black key.
They are called enharmonics.

Student Position
One Octave Higher When Performing as a Duet

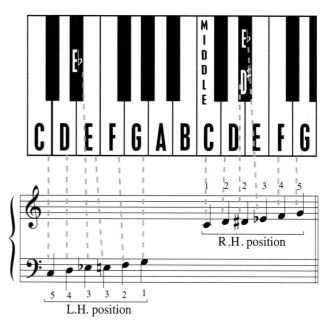

Ready, Set, Rock!
Optional Teacher Accompaniment

With energy

mf

Eric Baumgartner

Ready, Set, Rock!

Play both hands one octave higher when performing as a duet.

Eric Baumgartner

14

The Phrase

Groups of notes, like words in books, tell stories when they are arranged in 'sentences' and punctuated. A curved line over a group of notes indicates a MUSICAL SENTENCE called a PHRASE.

Student Position

One Octave Higher When Performing as a Duet

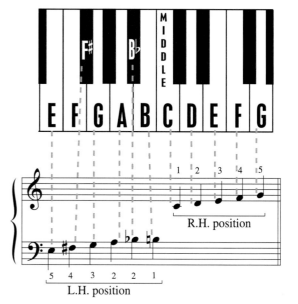

Blue Waltz

Optional Teacher Accompaniment

Eric Baumgartne

Moderate waltz tempo

mp

5

9

13

Blue Waltz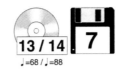

Play both hands one octave higher when performing as a duet.

Moderate waltz tempo

Eric Baumgartner

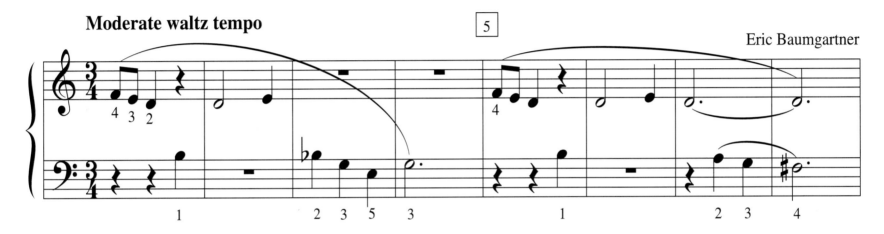

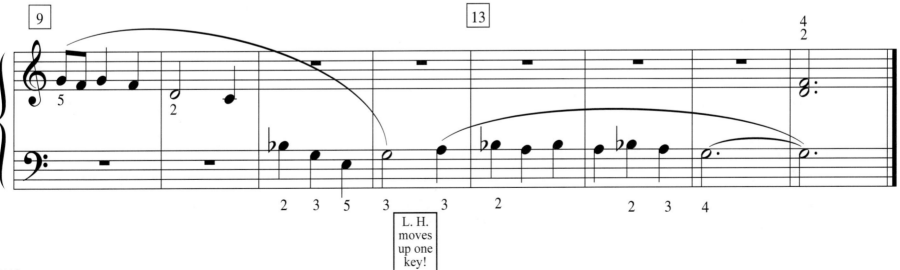

L. H.
moves
up one
key!

12418

Student Position
One Octave Higher When Performing as a Duet

D.C. al Fine
When you see this, go back to the beginning and play to the *Fine*.

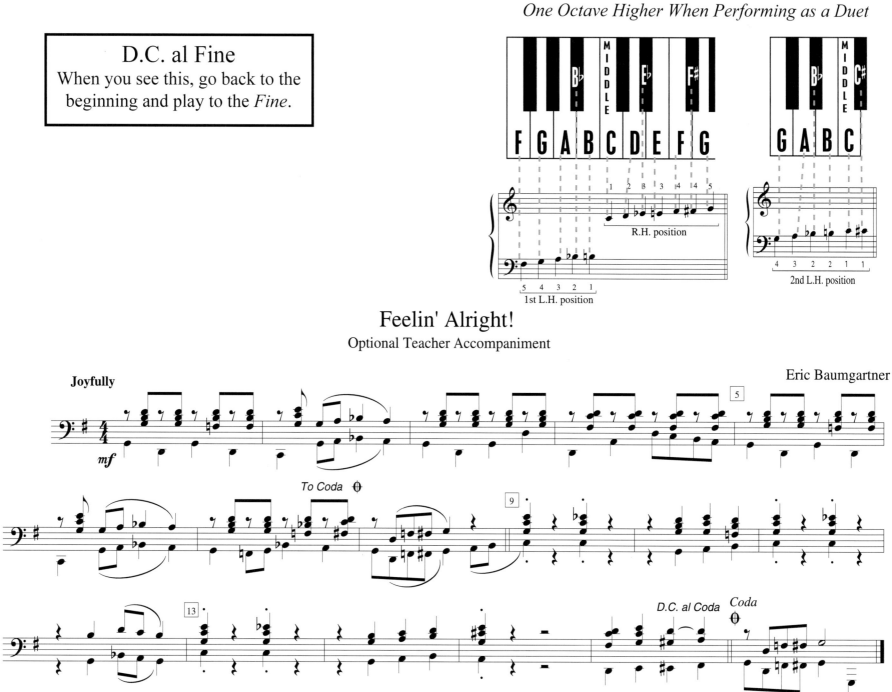

Feelin' Alright!
Optional Teacher Accompaniment

Eric Baumgartner

Feelin' Alright!

Play both hand one octave higher when performing as a duet.

Eric Baumgartner

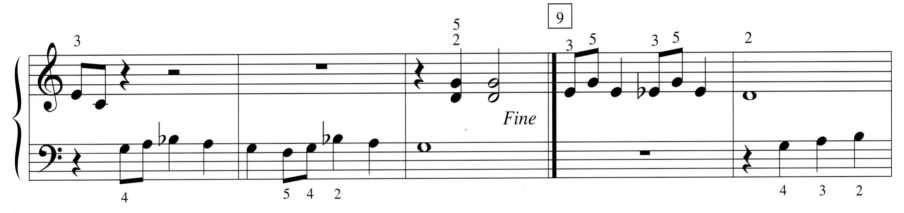

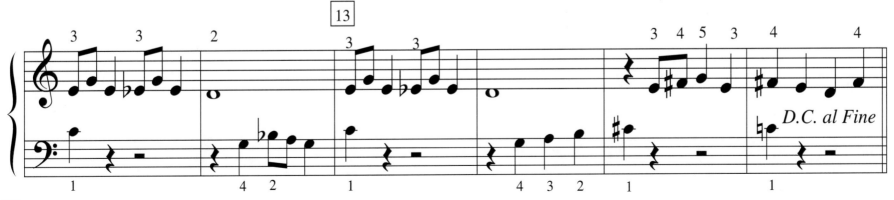

18

Scott Joplin

Joplin is known as the "King of Ragtime." Ragtime, an early type of jazz music, has had a big influence on the world of 'rock & roll'. The rhythms and harmonies of Joplin's music have influenced many composers in their style of

Student Position
One Octave Higher When Performing as a Duet

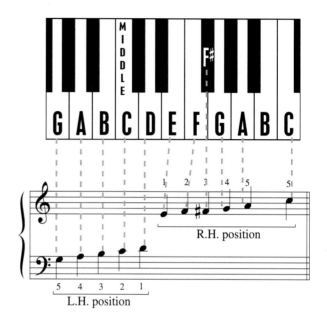

The Entertainer
Optional Teacher Accompaniment

Scott Joplin

arr. Eric Baumgartner

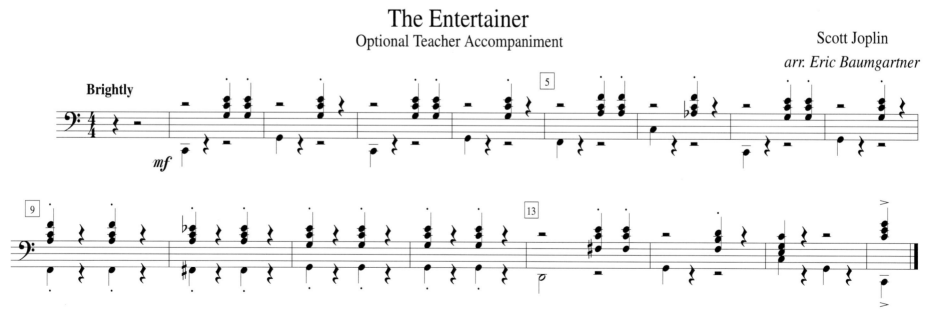

12418

The Entertainer
2nd Theme

Play both hands one octave higher when performing as a duet.

Scott Joplin
arr. Eric Baumgartner

Brightly

Rhythm Pattern
Only 2 patterns to know.

Get this and you've got it.

Student Position
One Octave Higher When Performing as a Duet

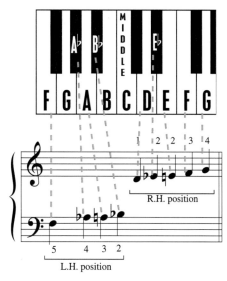

Jazz Chord Bop
Optional Teacher Accompaniment

Eric Baumgartner

Cool and relaxed

mf

Jazz Chord Bop

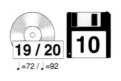

Play both hands one octave higher when performing as a duet.

Cool and relaxed

Eric Baumgartner

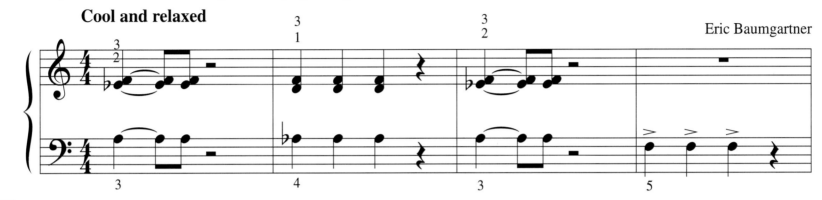

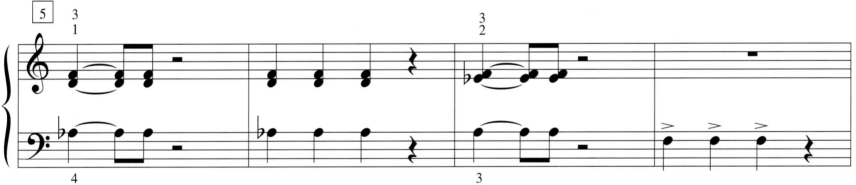

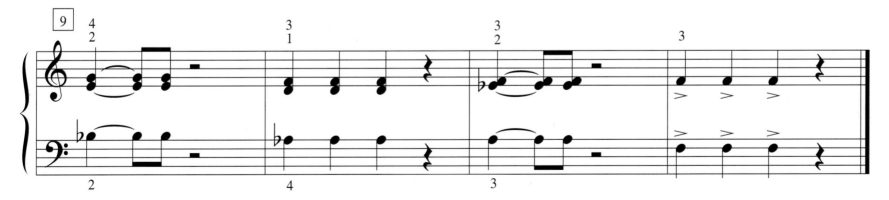

12418

Traffic Jam

Play as written when performing as a duet.

Eric Baumgartner

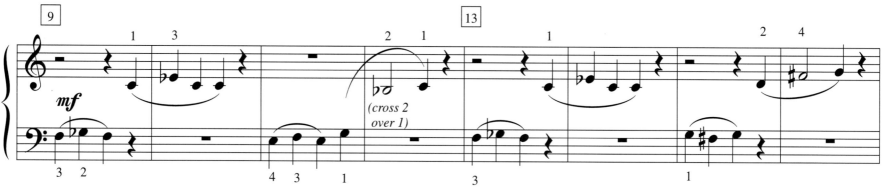

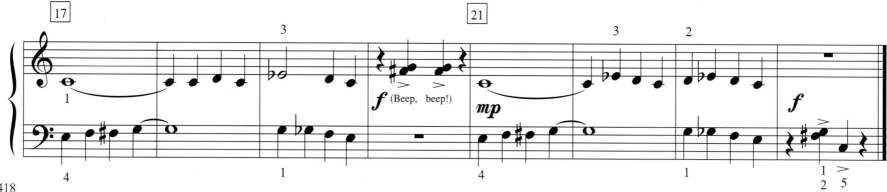

Play As Written When Performed as a Duet.

Dynamics

DYNAMICS are suggestions by the composer to help create contrasts in your music. In this piece you will find the *f*, meaning *loud,* the *mf*, meaning *medium loud,* and the *mp*, meaning *medium soft*.

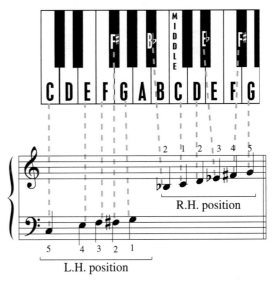

Traffic Jam
Optional Teacher Accompaniment

Eric Baumgartner

Briskly

mf

Teaching Little Fingers To Play....
EVERYTHING THEY **WANT** TO PLAY!

Starting from the very beginning with *Teaching Little Fingers To Play* by John Thompson and progressing through *Teaching Little Fingers To Play More* by Leigh Kaplan, students will enjoy practicing and performing these wonderful supplements!

If it's **FUN** to **PLAY**...
It's *Teaching Little Fingers*!